Origami

The Math Behind the Folds

By Amanda Onion

CELEBRATION PRESS
Pearson Learning Group

Contents

a drawing of three women folding origami

The Math Behind the Folds

What is origami? The answer is in the word. In Japanese, *ori* means "to fold" and *gami* means "paper." It's amazing what elaborate shapes you can make by folding a simple square of paper!

Origami shapes are called **models**, and the people who make the models are known as paper folders. People have been making origami models for a long time. It is believed that origami began almost 2,000 years ago in China. The craft was then brought to Japan. At the time origami was introduced to Japan, paper was considered very valuable.

Making shapes out of paper is not only fun, it's also a great way to learn math. For one thing, creating origami models shows you how certain shapes are made—and that can tell you a lot about **geometry**.

Practicing origami also teaches you about fractions. When you fold a piece of paper, you are **dividing** it into smaller parts.

In addition, origami teaches you about another kind of math: **algebra**. That's because for many models, whatever fold you make on one side, you make on the other.

This book will show you how to make some origami models ranging from easy to challenging. It will also demonstrate how math is behind every shape you make.

Getting Started

Here are some tips to keep in mind as you begin paper folding: To make neat shapes, fold your paper on a hard, flat surface, such as a table. Always check to see that your edges line up before pressing a fold. Once you've pressed a fold, you will leave a permanent crease in the paper, so you'll want to be sure your fold is correct. When you're sure the fold is correctly placed, use your fingers to press the crease firmly against the surface.

Basic Folds

There are two main folds in origami, the valley fold and the mountain fold. Learning how to make these folds is the first step to folding more complicated models.

VALLEY AND MOUNTAIN FOLDS

Materials: 2 square pieces of paper

VALLEY FOLD

A valley fold is a fold toward the front. To make a valley fold, take the far end of a piece of paper that is in front of you and fold it toward yourself.

When the paper is unfolded, the crease line in the paper forms a valley shape.

MOUNTAIN FOLD

A mountain fold is a fold toward the back. To make a mountain fold, take the near end of your paper and fold it away from you.

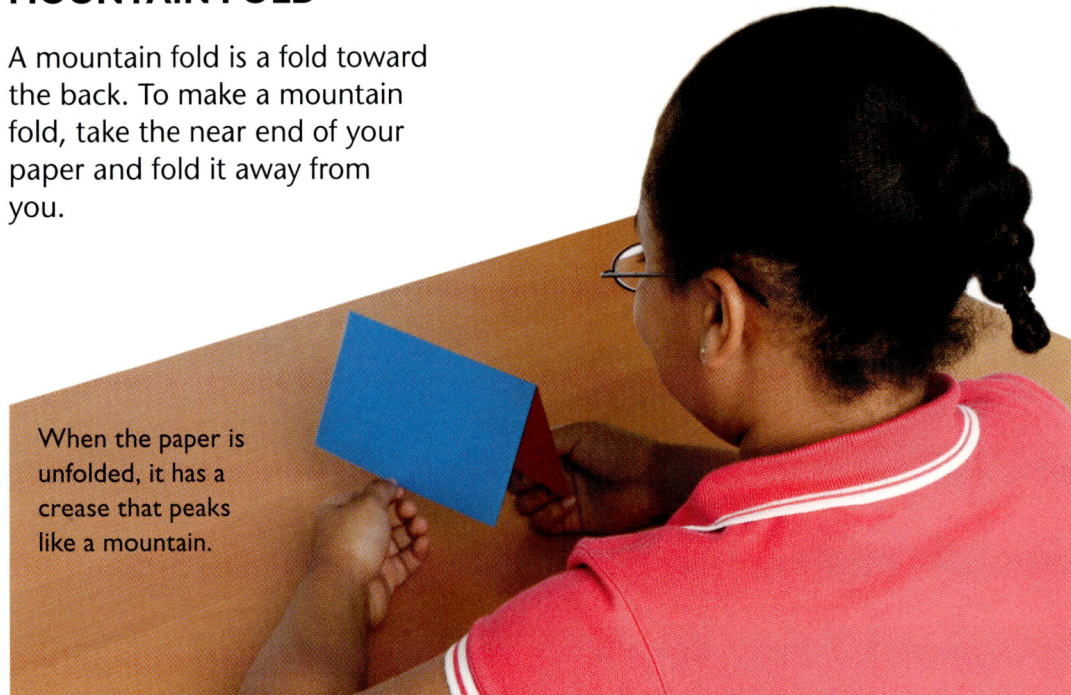

When the paper is unfolded, it has a crease that peaks like a mountain.

BEHIND THE FOLDS:
Square vs. Rectangle

Think about the geometry behind the folds you make. A rectangle is a shape in which opposite sides are equal in length and all angles are right angles. A square is a kind of rectangle where all four sides are equal in length. What happens to your paper's square shape when you make your folds?

Make a Samurai Helmet

Samurai warriors were famous fighters of ancient Japan who played an important role in defending farmers' land and the country of Japan. The top warriors led their lives according to a strict code. They were loyal, disciplined, and respectful of others. To be a samurai warrior was a great honor.

It took years of training to achieve the necessary skills. Samurai training included learning to move gracefully and to attack with skill and courage.

Samurai warriors fought with swords and other weapons, and they often wore **elaborate** armor, including helmets with horns. Now, you can fold a samurai helmet from paper.

a nineteenth-century print of a samurai warrior

SAMURAI HELMET

Level of Difficulty: Beginner

Materials: a large square piece of paper, colored on two sides (The bigger the square, the bigger the hat will be. A 12-inch square of paper will make a hat that will fit most heads.)

PROCEDURE

Fold the paper square in half, using a valley fold, to make a triangle.

Fold the triangle in half again, bringing the right point to the left point, to make a crease down the middle. Open it after creasing.

Fold the corners down, one at a time, to meet at the center crease.

Fold the bottom points up, using mountain folds, to touch the top point.

5

Then, fold back the points from the top middle, as shown, to create two even triangles.

6

top flap

bottom flap

Fold the top flap halfway up to the top point. Press to crease it down.

7

bottom edge

Fold the bottom edge up and press to crease along the fold.

8

Tuck the bottom flap behind the helmet to form the back of the helmet.

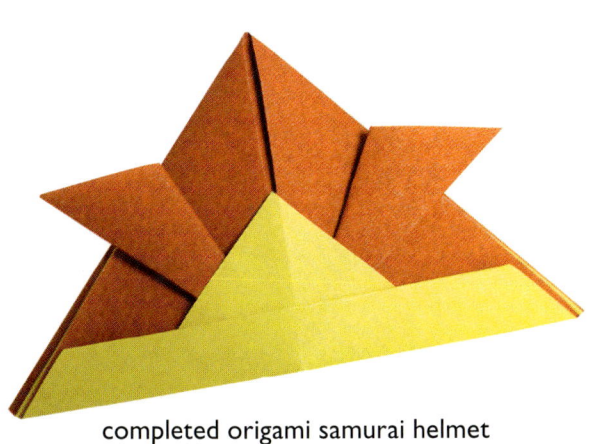

completed origami samurai helmet

a seventeenth-century samurai helmet

Make a Square Box

Now it's time to fold something practical—a box! You can even add a lid by making a second box with a bigger piece of paper. As you fold the box, think about how many different kinds of shapes you are making along the way.

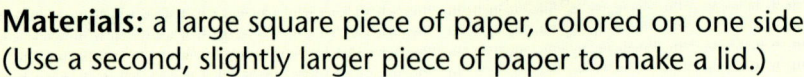

SQUARE BOX

Level of Difficulty: Intermediate

Materials: a large square piece of paper, colored on one side (Use a second, slightly larger piece of paper to make a lid.)

PROCEDURE

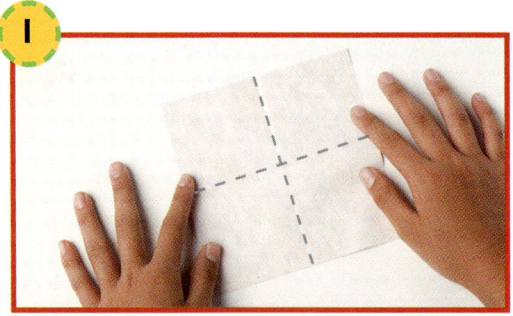

Fold your square piece of paper in half both ways so you have a center point.

Fold down a corner so that it meets the center point.

Fold the other three corners into the center.

4

Fold in the two sides so that they meet in the middle.

5

Unfold the two sides completely. Leave the other two corners folded in.

6

Fold in the two sides to the middle.

7

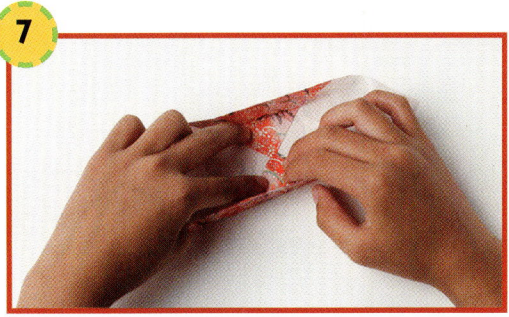

Then, let the sides flap out again. This forms two sides of the box.

8

To form the third side of the box, first push in at the two diagonal folds.

9

Then, pinch and crease both edges of the box.

10

Bring the end over the top and tuck it in neatly. Repeat steps 8–10 on the opposite side of the box.

To make a lid for the box, follow steps 1–10, using a larger piece of paper.

BEHIND THE FOLDS:
Fractions and Geometric Shapes

Think about the shapes you made as you folded your box. You began with a square. Then you folded it in half both ways and made four squares. Each small square was a fraction, or a part, of the original square. How big was each smaller square compared with the original, bigger square?

When you folded down the corners, you made four equal triangles. By folding in the sides in step 4, you made a rectangle. And when you unfolded the two sides in step 5, you made a hexagon. A hexagon is a figure with six sides.

a hexagon

Make a Star Box

Now that you have made a box and a lid, try folding a box that is a little more challenging to make. The star box makes a good gift container. Fill it with small items to give someone special.

As you fold, think about the different parts of a triangle. The base and two sides are the three lines that form the triangle's shape. The point of a triangle opposite the base is called the **apex**.

There are different kinds of triangles. A right triangle has a corner that is a right angle of 90 degrees. An isosceles triangle has two sides of equal length. It also has two angles that are equal in measurement. A scalene triangle has no sides that are of equal length and no equal angles. An **equilateral** triangle has three sides of equal length and three equal angles.

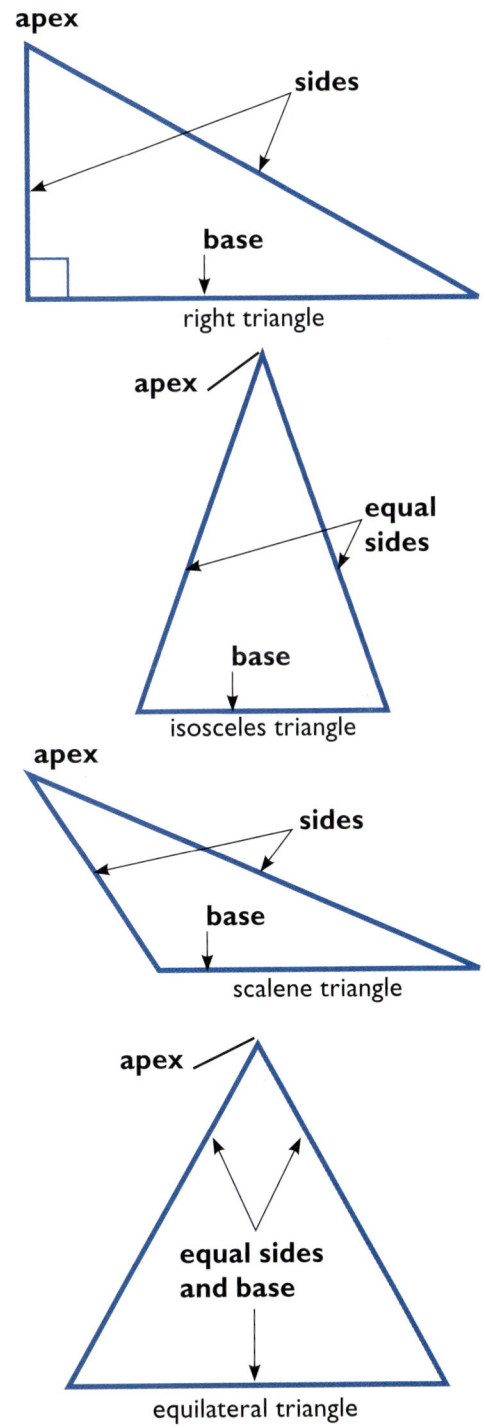

apex

sides

base

right triangle

apex

equal sides

base

isosceles triangle

apex

sides

base

scalene triangle

apex

equal sides and base

equilateral triangle

STAR BOX

Level of Difficulty: Advanced

Materials: a square piece of paper, colored on two sides

PROCEDURE

1

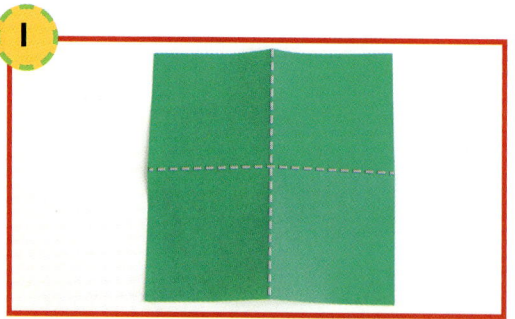

Fold your square piece of paper in half both ways. Open it up to reveal the creases down the middle.

2

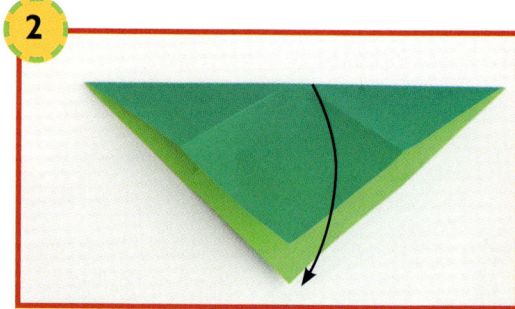

Position paper in front of you to look like a diamond. Then, fold paper in half into a triangle shape, using a valley fold.

3

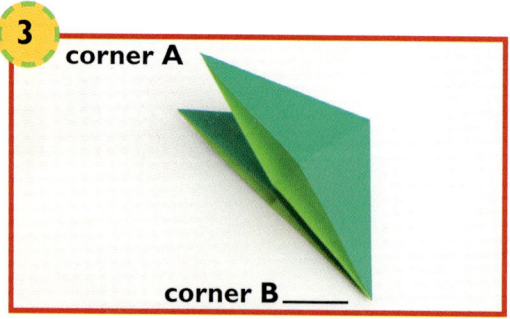

corner A

corner B

Fold the triangle in half again to form a smaller triangle.

4

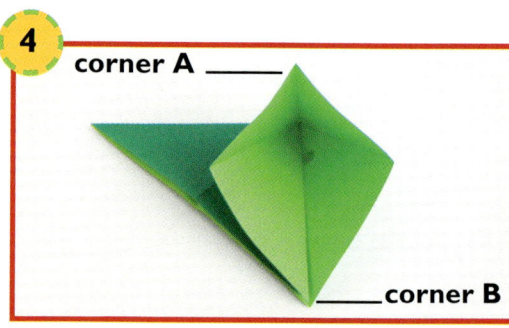

corner A _____

_____ corner B

Take corner A and lift toward the center.

5

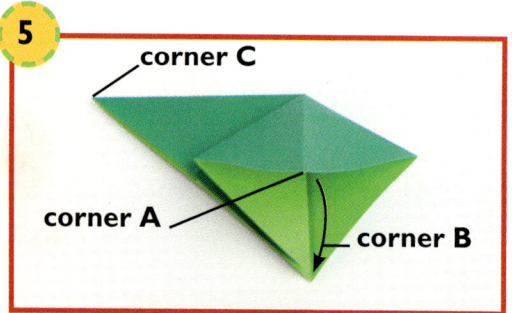

corner C

corner A

corner B

Then, using the creases created in steps 1 to 4 as a guide, bring down corner A to meet corner B.

6

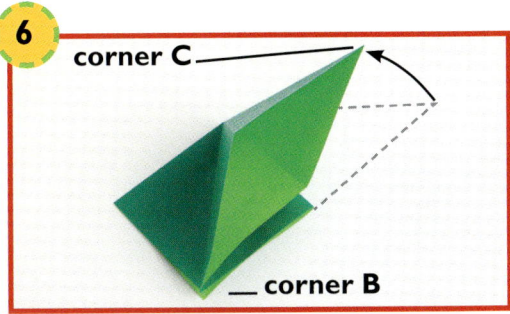

corner C

corner B

Turn paper over. Lift corner C to the center and bring down to meet corner B.

7

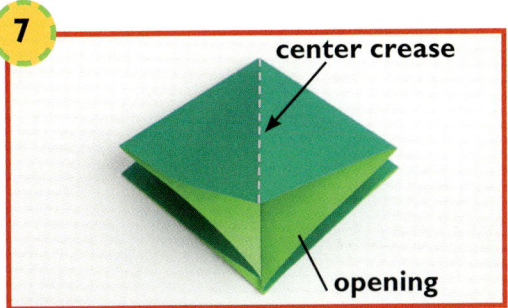

center crease

opening

This diamond shape is what you should have after step 6. Notice the center crease in the middle of the diamond.

8

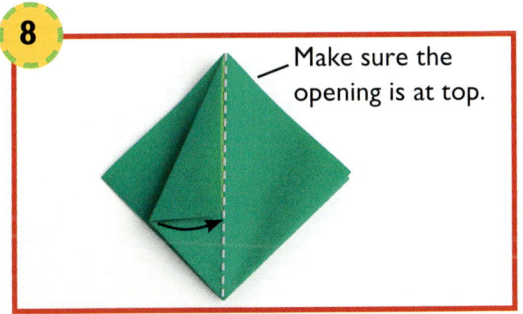

Make sure the opening is at top.

Rotate your diamond shape so the opening is at the top. Fold the left side to the center crease.

9

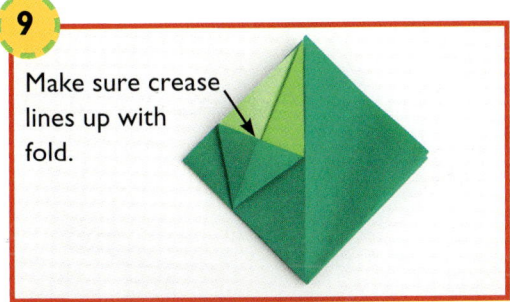

Make sure crease lines up with fold.

Open up the folded flap that you just made and press it flat. Make sure that the crease in the top area aligns with the fold.

10

Fold the left section of the flap behind itself.

11

Fold the right side to the center crease. Repeat steps 9 and 10 on the right side.

12

Both sides should look alike.

13

Turn the paper over and repeat steps 8 to 12 to the left and right sides. The back should look just like the front when you have finished.

14

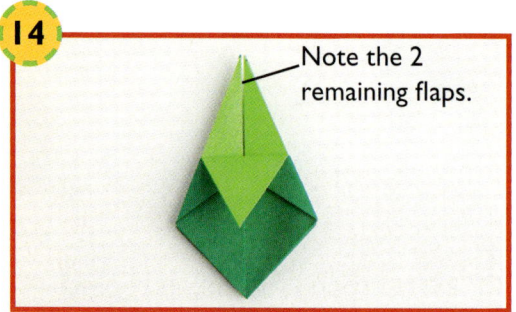

Note the 2 remaining flaps.

Fold down the flap as far as it can go. Turn the paper over and repeat on the other side.

15

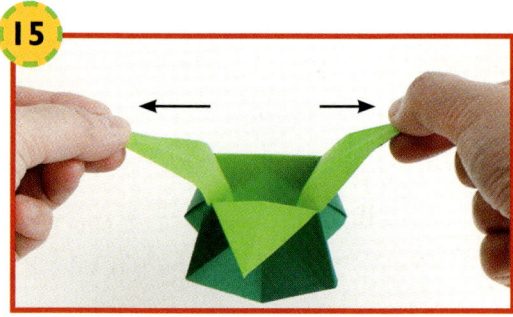

Then, gently pull the two remaining flaps out to open up your box.

16

Crease and flatten the two remaining flaps. Then, flatten out the bottom of the box.

Neaten up the star flaps and fill up your star box.

Make a Crane

Sometimes origami shapes take on special meaning. One example is the true story of a young Japanese girl named Sadako Sasaki. Sadako was two years old at the end of World War II when the Japanese city of Hiroshima was hit by an atomic bomb.

Nine years later, when she was eleven years old, Sadako fell ill with cancer as a result of being exposed to the bombing. When she heard about a Japanese legend that anyone who folds 1,000 origami cranes is granted her heart's desire, Sadako began folding.

During fourteen months in a hospital, Sadako folded more than 1,300 cranes. Still, she died at the age of twelve. It's a sad story, but many children remember her by folding paper cranes in her memory. You can remember Sadako, too, as you make your own crane.

The instructions on the following pages show you how to fold a paper crane. As you fold, think about how many times you are dividing your piece of paper.

a memorial to Sadako Sasaki

PAPER CRANE

Level of Difficulty: Expert

Materials: a square piece of paper, colored on two sides

PROCEDURE

1

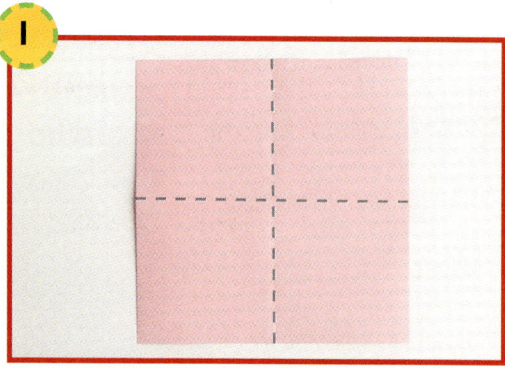

Fold your square piece of paper in half both ways. Unfold the paper back to a square.

2

Rotate paper in front of you to look like a diamond. Then, fold paper in half into a triangle shape, using a valley fold.

3

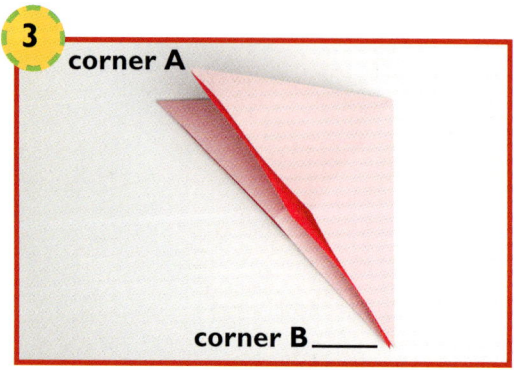

corner A

corner B_____

Fold the triangle in half again to form a smaller triangle.

4

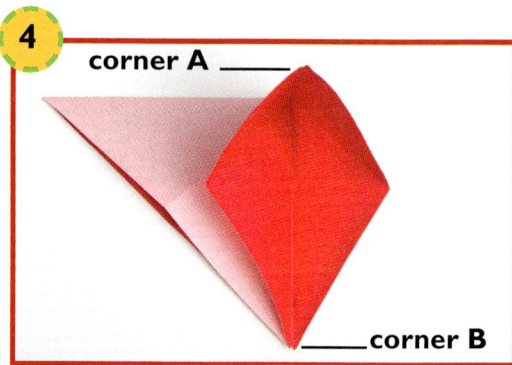

corner A _____

_____corner B

Take corner A and lift it up toward the center.

5

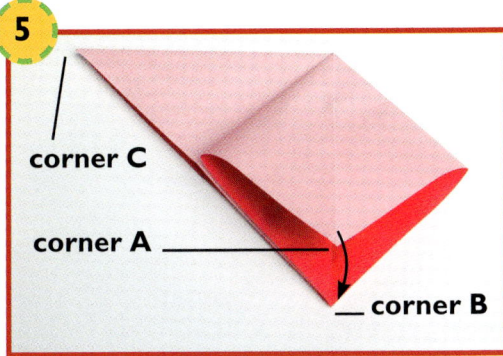

corner C

corner A

corner B

Then, using the creases created in steps 1 to 4, bring down corner A to meet corner B and press folds.

6

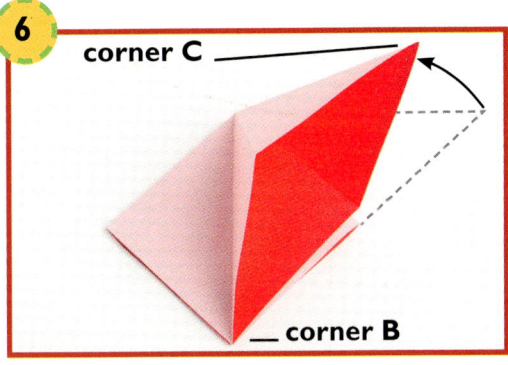

corner C

corner B

Turn paper over and lift corner C to the center and bring down to meet corner B and press folds.

7

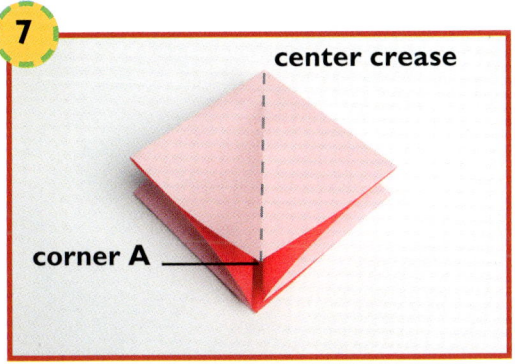

center crease

corner A

This diamond shape is what you should have after step 6. Notice the center crease in the middle of the diamond.

8

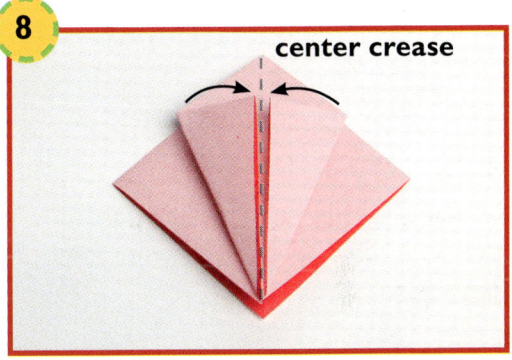

center crease

Fold in the outer corners to meet the center crease. Turn the paper over. Repeat on the other side. This step creates the side creases.

9

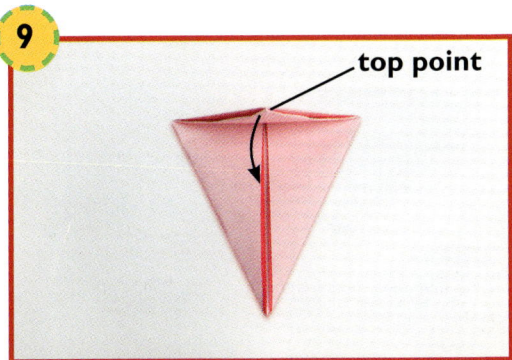

top point

Fold the top point where the outer corners meet. This creates the top crease. Unfold your folds back to the diamond shape in step 7.

10

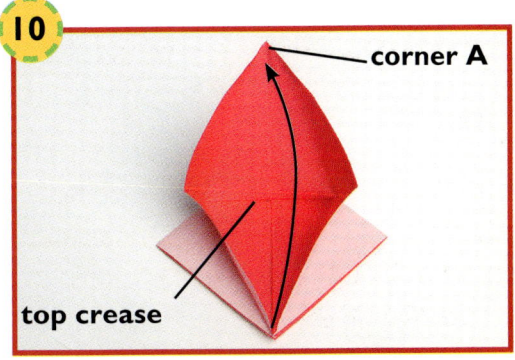

corner A

top crease

Lift up corner A (which is labeled in step 7) until the paper bends at the top crease.

19

11

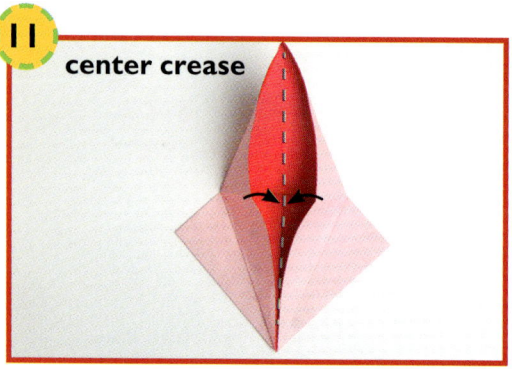

center crease

Then, fold in the sides, using the side creases as your guide, to meet at the center crease. Turn over and repeat on the other side.

12

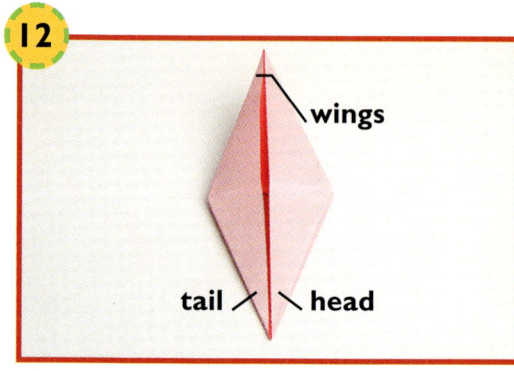

wings

tail   head

This diamond is the shape you should have. The bottom section of the diamond is the neck and the tail. The top section is the wings.

13

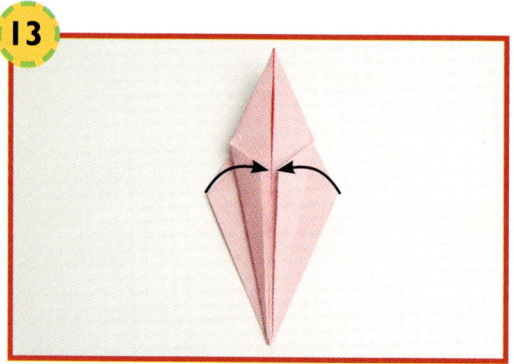

Fold in the outside corners to meet the center crease. Turn over and repeat on the other side.

14

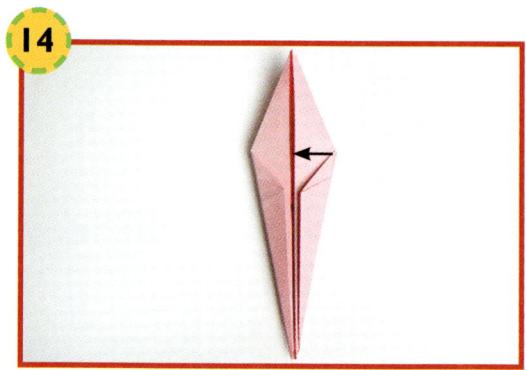

Fold the top flap in the direction of the arrow. Turn over and repeat on the other side.

15

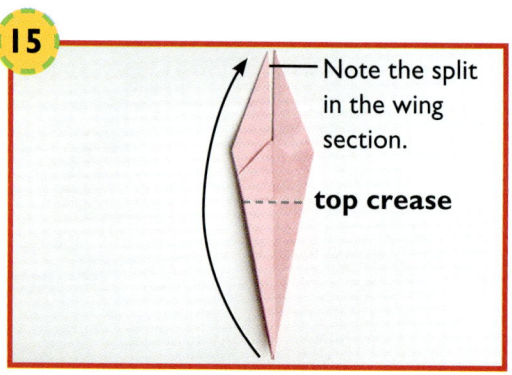

Note the split in the wing section.

top crease

Fold up the head and tail section at the top crease. Repeat on the other side.

16

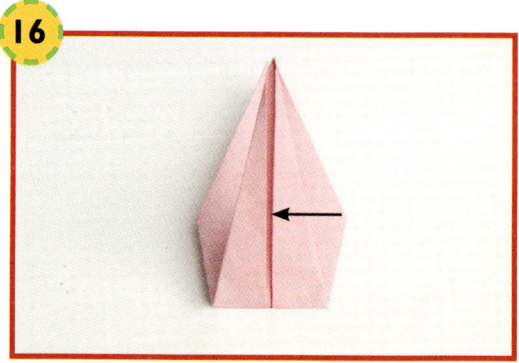

Fold the wing flap in the direction of the arrow. Turn over and repeat on the other side.

17

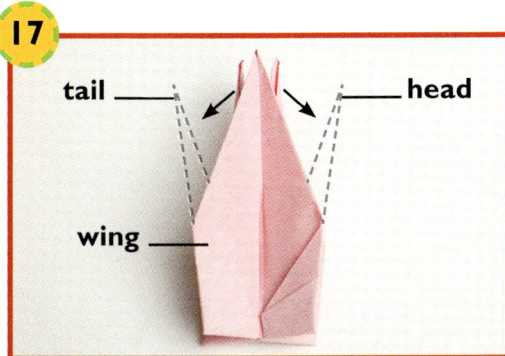

tail — head

wing —

Your crane should look like this.
Gently pull the neck and tail out and
down, as shown by the dotted lines.

18

Bend the top portion down to create
the head. Gently pull wings straight
out to inflate the body. You can
also blow through the hole at the
underside of the crane.

BEHIND THE FOLDS:
Symmetry

Your finished crane is an example of symmetry.
One-half of the figure is the mirror image of the
other half. If you unfold the head of your crane,
you can see how it mirrors the tail. The crane's
two wings are also symmetrical. The model is
symmetrical because as you folded the crane,
you made the same folds on two sides.

Origami: A Skill for Many Trades

It's possible to make origami models of almost all things, including animals, plants, and buildings—and even people. Some paper folders make mathematical models. Others specialize in modular origami, where many copies of a folded shape are assembled to form larger structures.

Paper folders include a wide group of people such as artists, scientists, mathematicians, therapists, and even engineers. Mathematicians use origami to help understand **equations**. Therapists can use origami to help people relax and work through their problems. Some engineers use origami to find the best way to fold air bags inside automobiles. Can you think of why origami might be useful for other kinds of jobs?

Origami shows that with a little imagination and skill, and some math behind the folds, you can do so much with a simple piece of paper.

It took 30 pieces of origami paper to create this model!

Glossary

algebra a kind of math in which letters representing numbers are combined according to the rules of math

apex the highest point or tip of something

dividing separating into parts, sections, groups, or branches

elaborate intricate and rich in detail; planned with attention to numerous parts or details

equations statements asserting the equality of two expressions

equilateral a geometric figure in which all of the sides are equal in length

geometry the mathematics of the properties, measurement, and relationships of points, lines, angles, surfaces, and solids

models small objects that represent in detail other, often larger objects

Index

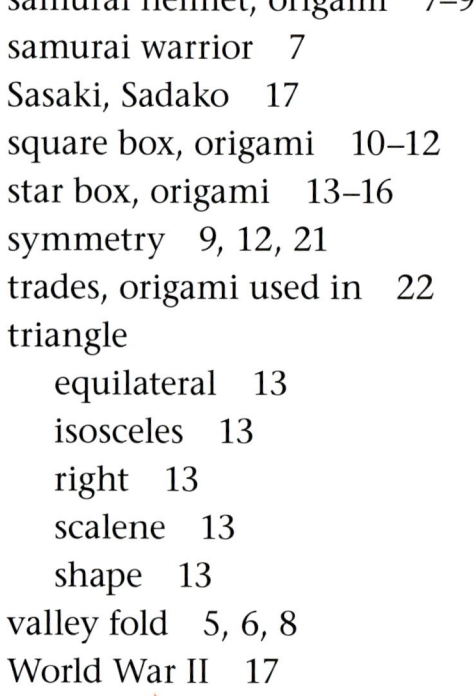